Oil Spills!

The Perils of Petroleum

by Jane Duden and Susan Walker

Perfection Learning® CA

Cover Photo: NOAA HAZMAT
Book Design: Randy Messer
Inside Illustration: Mike Aspengren, Kay Ewald (maps)
Some images copyright www.arttoday.com
Photographs courtesy of Charlie Crangle: pp 6, 18, 19, 25–33, 45, 54, 55.
Photographs provided courtesy of NOAA Digital Image Archiving and
   Access, an ESDIM-funded project: pp 3, 5, 9, 14, 16, 17, 20, 22, 34.

About the Authors

Jane Duden is a former elementary teacher in Minnesota and Germany. As a freelance writer, Ms. Duden has written 28 nonfiction books for children. She writes for teachers and kids on many topics but with great enthusiasm for animals, science, and the environment. Her quest for stories and adventures has taken her to every continent, including Antarctica. At home, she likes cooking, swimming, biking, in-line skating, and learning new things. She enjoys speaking at schools because she likes the spirit and sharing of young authors.

Jane lives in Minneapolis with a houseful of pets.

Susan Walker is a teacher and writer. She loves children's books, and this is her first one. Susan has taught children from kindergarten to 12th grade. She loves to learn all the new things her students have to teach her.

Susan lives in Moose Pass, Alaska, with her husband, Todd, and three yellow labs, Jestic, Elmo and Butch. Living in Alaska helped her to experience the people and places that helped to add real life to this book. She was also able to see firsthand the kind of dedication and commitment the people of a community so selflessly put forth after an oil-spill disaster.

When she is not writing or teaching, Susan loves to hike, fish, and cook.

Table of Contents

NOAA HAZMAT photo

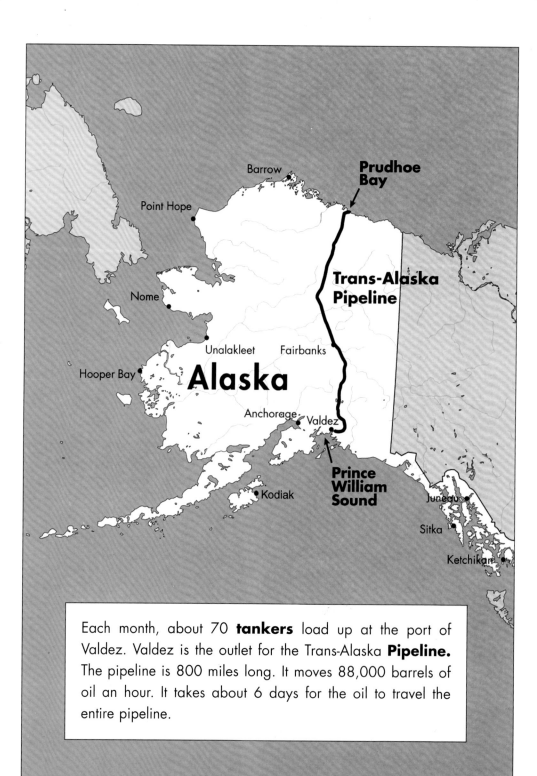

Each month, about 70 **tankers** load up at the port of Valdez. Valdez is the outlet for the Trans-Alaska **Pipeline.** The pipeline is 800 miles long. It moves 88,000 barrels of oil an hour. It takes about 6 days for the oil to travel the entire pipeline.

Disaster!

It was just before midnight. The *Exxon Valdez* slid safely through the dangerous narrows of Prince William Sound. It was fully loaded with 170,000 tons of **crude oil.** The oil had come through the Trans-Alaska Pipeline from Prudhoe Bay. And it was headed for oil **refineries** in Washington state.

A local pilot had come aboard to guide the ship. He was an expert in local waters. And he'd done his job well. As usual, he got off the *Exxon Valdez* and returned to shore when his work was complete.

Now the *Exxon Valdez* had just one more turn. But it takes a long time to turn such a big ship.

Suddenly, the deck officer saw the flashing red light. It was the warning light on rocky Bligh Reef. He knew the ship wasn't going to make the turn.

Steel screeched on stone. The tanker slammed onto the reef. It shuddered to a halt. The alarm bell split the night air. Thick, black crude oil gushed from the torn hull.

The worst oil spill in U.S. history was underway.

NOAA HAZMAT photo

Chapter

Major Oil Spills

The Wreck of the *Exxon Valdez*

On March 24, 1989, the people of Alaska awoke to a nightmare. Millions of gallons of crude Alaskan oil had blackened the clean water of Prince William Sound.

Prince William Sound, Alaska

The crippled *Exxon Valdez* lay grounded on the rocks. The smell of oil was overpowering. Thousands of birds, otters, seals, and other animals were dead or dying.

News of the disaster spread. Dozens of airplanes circled overhead. People were stunned, angry, frustrated, and sad. Prince William Sound was a place they loved and treasured. They rushed to do whatever they could.

But 11 million gallons of crude oil had flooded into the water. Sea life, beaches, wildlife, fisheries, and families would never be the same.

> **How much is 11 million gallons?**
>
> It would be equal to the oil drained from 8.8 million cars. And it would fill up
> - 3 ½ school gyms
> - 44 high school swimming pools,
> - and 92 average houses.

Cleanup began. Volunteers worked. People from Exxon worked. Leaders came from the U.S. Coast Guard. They came from state and federal agencies. They came from all over the world.

But the *Exxon Valdez* spill was about 175 times larger than anyone was prepared to handle. No one had enough equipment. And nobody had a way to organize it fast.

Prince William Sound was a remote area with few roads. It was hard to deliver all the oil-pickup gear needed. Some was dropped by planes at the spill.

Only the fishermen knew the tides and currents. And only the fishermen had boats for rescue work.

By the time everyone got into gear, the weather turned bad. Nature changed the course of this disaster. Windstorms broke up the **slick.** Oil spread far and wide. The *Exxon Valdez* showed the world just how deadly an oil spill can be.

From 1973 to 1993, there were 200,000 oil spills in U.S. waters. That's an average of 28 spills a day. That equals 31,000 gallons of oil spilled every day for 20 years.

> **How much is in one barrel of oil ?**
>
> 1 barrel = 42 U.S. gallons
> 1 ton = approximately 7½ barrels or 315 gallons

Other Spills

From 1980 to 1988, tankers in the U.S. had 468 **groundings,** 37 **collisions,** 97 **rammings,** 55 fires and explosions, and 95 deaths. Each time, oil spilled onto land or into water.

Many oil tankers go to Washington state. In 1985, a huge spill took place. The *Arco Anchorage,* filled with Alaskan crude oil, turned off course. The water was too shallow for the heavy tanker. It ran aground, spilling 239,000 gallons of oil. This was the largest spill in Washington history. The oil killed thousands of sea birds.

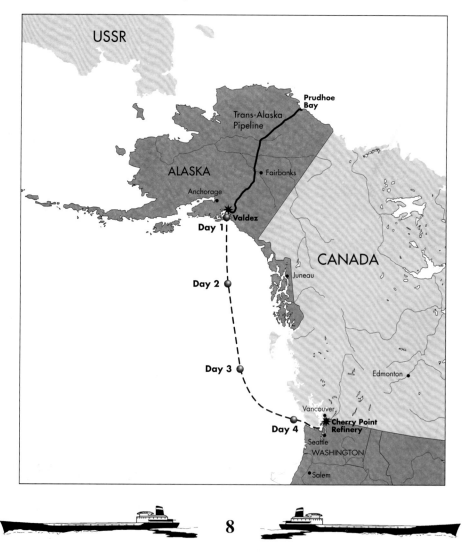

NOAA HAZMAT photo

In 1993, three ships collided at the entrance to Tampa Bay, Florida. One exploded and caught fire. The ships spilled about 328,000 gallons of oil. A 17-mile oil slick formed on the water.

In January 1997, oil spilled into the Sea of Japan. It happened when the *Nakhodka* broke apart in stormy seas. At least 133,000 barrels of fuel spilled. Japan worked hard to rescue sea life and keep the oil from damaging beaches and wildlife. The oil coated 560 miles of coast. It hurt shellfish farms, scenic beaches, and sea bird sanctuaries.

In 1997, oil spilled in Alaska again. The **freighter** *Kuroshima* lost its **anchor** during a fierce storm. It crashed into a rock. Nearly 80,000 gallons streamed into Dutch Harbor.

This ship was not a tanker. The spilled oil was its fuel. The fuel floated on the water and covered the beaches. It got so thick it could be cut like fudge.

Spills don't happen just at sea. In 1988, a 4-million-gallon oil storage tank split apart. The tank was in Floreffe, Pennsylvania. It cracked while being filled with oil. The oil flowed over a parking lot and into a storm drain. This drain emptied into the Monongahela River, which emptied into the Ohio River.

Within minutes, the oil had **polluted** drinking water for 1 million people in three states. It killed wildlife. It damaged people's property. It hurt businesses.

In January 1990, an Exxon pipe broke in New York City. Thousands of gallons of heating oil spilled into water near a bird sanctuary.

In 1993, a pipeline in Fairfax County, Virginia, broke. Over 400,000 gallons of oil spilled before the pipeline could be shut down. The oil affected a creek and the Potomac River.

The *Exxon Valdez* spill was the largest single spill in American waters. It was an **ecological** disaster like no other.

But other spills have been even bigger. Of the world's largest oil spills from 1967–1992, *Exxon Valdez* ranked 36.

You probably haven't heard about most oil spills—just the really big ones. That's because spills that affect coastlines, people, wildlife, and jobs do the most harm. They cost more money. They affect more people. And they make more headlines.

Here are some other big oil spills at sea.

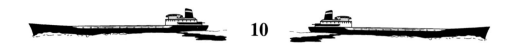

10 Largest Tanker Spills in the World

Map	Date	Tanker	Location	Gallons spilled	Cause
1	8/6/83	*Castillo de Bellver*	Capetown, South Africa	79 million	Breakup, fire, sinking
2	3/16/78	*Amoco Cadiz*	Brittany, France	68 million	Grounding
3	7/19/79	*Atlantic Empress*	North of Tobago	43 million	Collision, explosion, fire
4	2/23/80	*Irene's Serenade*	Pilos, Greece	37 million	Explosion, fire, sinking
5	12/19/72	*Sea Star*	Gulf of Oman	36 million	Collision
6	3/18/67	*Torrey Canyon*	Isles of Scilly, U.K.	36 million	Grounding
7	2/25/77	*Hawaiian Patriot*	West of Honolulu, Hawaii	31 million	Explosion, fire
8	5/12/76	*Urquiola*	La Corua, Spain	30 million	Grounding, explosion
9	3/2/70	*Othello*	Vaxholm, Sweden	30 million	Collision
10	11/15/79	*Independentza*	Istanbul, Turkey	29 million	Collision, explosion, fire

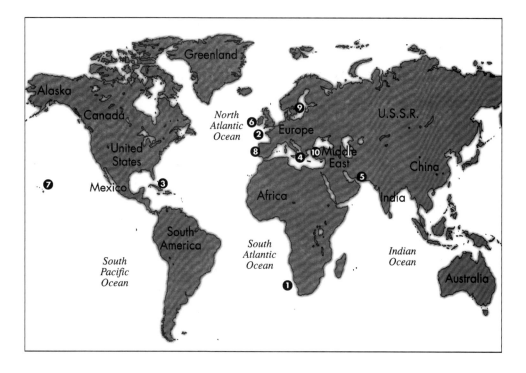

9 Largest Oil Spills By Tankers in U.S. Waters
(Spills over 1 million gallons since 1971)

Map	Date	Tanker	Location	Gallons spilled	Cause
1	3/24/89	*Exxon Valdez*	Prince William Sound, AK	11.1 million	Grounding
2	11/1/79	*Burmah Agate*	Galveston Bay, TX	10.7 million	Collision, fire, explosion
3	3/27/71	*Texaco Oklahoma*	North Carolina	9.0 million	Split in half
4	12/15/76	*Argo Merchant*	Southeast Massachusetts	7.6 million	Grounding
5	7/30/84	*Alvenus*	Cameron, LA	2.8 million	Grounding
6	10/31/84	*Puerto Rican*	San Francisco, CA	1.0 million	Explosion, fire
7	3/31/82	*Arkas*	Montz, LA	1.5 million	Collision, fire
8	11/20/80	*Georgia*	Pilottown, LA	1.3 million	Holed by anchor chain
9	1/28/81	*Olympic Glory*	Galveston Bay, TX	1.0 million	Collision

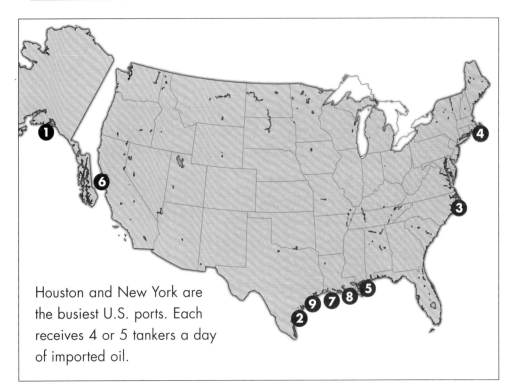

Houston and New York are the busiest U.S. ports. Each receives 4 or 5 tankers a day of imported oil.

How Do Oil Spills Happen?

Many things cause oil spills. The National Research Council (N.R.C.) studies spills and their causes.

How much oil is spilled in the world's oceans and waterways each year? The N.R.C. guesses about 1 billion gallons.

As bad as tanker spills can be, they are just 13 percent of the total oil lost. Oil gets into oceans other ways, like leaking pipelines and storage tanks. **Industry** and city wastes also contribute. Oil also gets spilled when tankers load and unload.

In the early 1970s, tanker crews dumped crude oil into the ocean as they cleaned ships. So much oil was spilled, it was considered the world's worst oil **pollution.**

Finally, oil shippers everywhere made changes. They changed the way tankers were cleaned. They made new fire-prevention rules. (Crude oil is very explosive.) And they used better **navigation** equipment.

New laws also made conditions better for crews. The laws were needed. Some crews worked 90 hours a week. Sometimes, their only sleep was two-hour naps. A tired, overworked crew makes more mistakes. Then accidents are more likely to happen.

These laws helped. But storms, earthquakes, lightning, fire, explosions, and collisions cause tanker accidents too.

And the way tankers are built can make spills worse. Single *hulls,* or bottoms, are blamed for many spills. There is just a single layer of steel separating the oil and the ocean. That layer is only 1 1/2 inches thick!

Like the *Exxon Valdez*, the *Arco Anchorage* had a single hull. Three years after the Arco spill, a Japanese tanker ran aground near the same place. But this ship had a **double hull.** And it spilled no oil. Some say a double hull would have meant much less oil spilled from the *Exxon Valdez.*

But tanker accidents are just one cause of oil spills. The Oil Spill Intelligence Report says that U.S. pipelines spill more oil than tanker accidents. Oil industry leaders say tankers and **barges** aren't all to blame. U.S. Navy ships, fishing boats, big cruise ships, and freighters spill less oil. But they spill more often. So do industrial plants. So do people who change oil in their cars. They pour old motor oil into drainage ditches, streams, and rivers. But just one major tanker spill can top all the routine spills in a decade.

One of the World's Worst Spills

Sometimes oil is spilled on purpose. This happened in 1991 in the Persian Gulf.

Many countries in the Middle East are rich in oil. In 1991, the leader of Iraq invaded Kuwait and took over its oil. The U.S., Britain, France, and several other countries attacked Iraq. They wanted to free Kuwait.

Iraq's leader, Saddam Hussein, would not give up Kuwait. He fought back with missiles and bombs.

Hussein even used oil as a weapon. He set fire to 700 oil wells. Oily smoke and poisons poured into the air. He opened oil pipelines in Kuwait. The oil gushed into the water of the Persian Gulf. In all, 250 million gallons of oil spilled.

The flood of thick oil covered beaches and water. It killed fish, water birds, and plants.

The flow spread. It threatened the drinking water for millions of people. Since much of Saudi Arabia is a desert, some cities get their water from the Persian Gulf.

Special factories, called **desalination** plants, remove salt from seawater. This makes the water fit to drink. Large, floating curtains called **booms** were used to enclose the oil spill. Booms and good winds kept the oil slick away from the desalination plants. But damage to the Gulf waters was still being studied long after the spill.

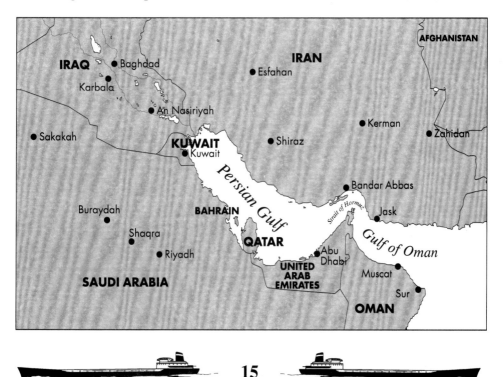

Chapter 2

After a Spill

The Life of an Oil Spill

Just five days after the *Exxon Valdez* spill, a 45-mile oil slick had formed.

As soon as an oil slick forms, it starts to change. Small amounts of oil spread from the main slick like fingers. It looks like a rainbow shining on the water. This sheen is light. And it evaporates quickly. But it can be deadly to birds and sea life.

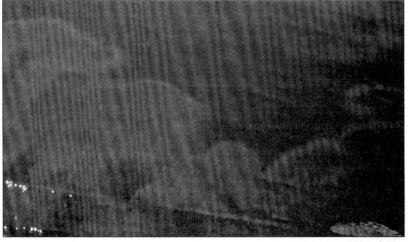

NOAA HAZMAT photo

Other light parts of the oil dissolve. They break into tiny droplets that mix with water.

Then the heaviest parts of the oil remain. The slick gets gooey. Waves stir up the thick mixture. This action forms a heavy water-in-oil mix.

Later, wind and waves slice the mix into pancake-like pieces. These break into tar balls that may wash ashore.

Sunlight and **bacteria** break down spilled oil. But all this happens at nature's pace. When oil is spilled, fast action saves lives, land, and water. We have learned ways to speed up the cleanup.

NOAA HAZMAT photo

Cleaning Up

Scientists have had lots of practice cleaning up oil spills. They have tried many ways of cleaning oil from water. They know what steps to take.

They try to keep the oil from spreading. They collect it and store it until the water can be removed. Then they **recycle** or safely dispose of the oil.

Scientists are always looking for new ways to clean up oil spills. But the basic ways have not changed. This is how they work:

Special Equipment

The first goal is to keep a spill from spreading. This helps limit the area damaged. Machines can help contain the spill.

Booms are laid on the water. Booms enclose the spill. They keep the oil together until it can be collected by pumps and **skimmers.**

Large, floating skimmer boats herd the oil together. The skimmer boats use special tools to suck the oily mixture into large containers.

After the mixture sits for a while, the oil and water separate. The water is removed. The oil is there. But now it is safely contained.

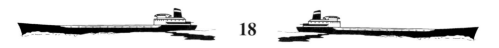

Pads help fight oil spills too. Pads work on beaches and in water that is too shallow for skimmer boats.

Workers lay strings of pads on the water's surface. These pads soak up the oil like paper towels. The oil-soaked pads go through a wringer that squeezes out the oil. Later, some of this oil can be recycled.

How many Kleenex?

It would take about 332 million boxes of Kleenex to soak up 11 million gallons of oil. That's how much oil spilled from the *Exxon Valdez!*

Hoses and shovels help clean oil. Workers shovel up oily sand and take it away. Sometimes, water is sprayed on rocks and oily sand. The spray forces the oil back into the water. Then booms and skimmers pick it up.

Fire

Thick oil floating on water can be burned. Fresh oil burns best. Burning can remove up to 98 percent of a fresh spill.

Special equipment and trained workers are needed. Crude oil is hard to set fire to. The smoke pollutes the air. And there is always the danger of unwanted fires.

Chemicals

Chemicals can be sprayed on oil. They help break oil down into tiny drops that dissolve in water. These chemicals speed up what wind and water do naturally.

Other chemicals help floating crude oil sink to the bottom. Or they make it stick together for easier pick-up. But chemicals can cause as much pollution as oil.

These methods work best for spills at sea. Chemicals, booms, and skimmers must be used before wind and waves spread the slick. But sometimes wind and water can help the cleanup.

Help from Nature

Over time, wind and waves break oil into droplets. These droplets mix with water and dissolve.

In 1979, the Ixtoc 1 oil well in the Gulf of Mexico blew up. This was a huge spill. It was about 140 million gallons!

Water and waves helped clean it up. Ocean winds and currents kept the slicks from drifting to shore. The oil spread out and broke down in the open sea.

Microbes are tiny plants or animals. Some of them can "eat" oil.

Microbes can change oil into harmless products like **carbon dioxide** and water. Microbes can get into the tiny spaces between soil. When conditions are right, they can live off the oil. They clean the pollution as they go.

Many microbes are needed to clean oil spills. By adding certain **fertilizers,** scientists make these microbes grow faster. Large numbers of microbes can feed on the oil until it disappears. Then their numbers go back to normal.

Microbes usually just clean up oily soil and small amounts of water. But experts used them with the *Exxon Valdez* cleanup. Fertilized microbes made the cleanup three to five times faster.

How tiny are microbes?

If the eraser on your pencil was a microbe, a drop of water would be the size of a football stadium.

What Happens to the Oil ?

Oil collected by skimmers and pumps is stored. Then it is treated and recycled. A wringer squeezes out oil-soaked pads. Some of this oil is also recycled. Oil-covered sand and gravel may be used in building roads. Oiled rags and clothing can be washed. Some oiled waste is burned. But most waste from oil spills is buried.

NOAA HAZMAT photo

The Alaska State Chemistry Laboratory had a new idea. After the *Exxon Valdez* spill, the lab had 2,000 samples of crude oil. It would have cost $6,000 to safely dispose of them. So they decided to sell the samples. They sold the oil in tiny bottles. The bottles cost under $10. The samples were not pure crude oil. They included rocks, seawater, or beach junk.

What did people do with the samples? Maybe they kept them as souvenirs. Profits go to finding the sources of oil spills. Then the right people can be held responsible for cleanup.

Changing Times:
Cleanup Methods for the 21st Century

Even with all these methods, oil cleanup is not foolproof. Every method has pros and cons. Experts keep searching. They want fast, Earth-friendly ways to clean up oil. So what's new in oil cleanup?

Elastol is one new idea. Elastol is a substance that comes from chewing gum. It makes oil turn into a thick layer—like the skin on hot chocolate. This layer gets dragged off water, then recycled.

Experts say that the oil-recovery rate could reach 97 percent by using this substance. Elastol works. It got rid of oil that seeped into a Brooklyn creek for many years.

Oats are another new oil-spill cleaner. Chemists at a skin-care company had the idea. They knew that oats could soak up the oil from skin. So why not from an oil slick?

They made a special recipe. It contained treated oat *pellets,* or tiny rocks. These pellets are spread out by tides. They are tasty treats for microbes. The microbes then "eat up" the slick.

Special thin glass beads also help. Scientists coat these beads with a substance that's also found in pudding mix. The beads are sprinkled on a spill. Then the sun changes the oil-coated beads into carbon dioxide and water. This leaves only sand behind.

All these methods work. Still, some oil always gets away. It is impossible to clean up all the oil from a spill. So what are the effects of oil spills?

Chapter

Deadly Lessons:
The Effects of an Oil Spill

The *Exxon Valdez*

The *Exxon Valdez* spill held our attention for weeks. We saw that deadly things can happen when tankers move oil. This chapter tells about rescue and cleanup after North America's largest oil spill. But the same things can happen anywhere that oil spills.

Effects on Beaches and Shorelines

People scooped and mopped oil for days and nights on end. They picked up oily seaweed. They tied up rocks in special bags so the tides could wash them. They searched for dead and dying wildlife. They picked them up before other animals could eat them and be poisoned. They wiped rocks by hand. They shoveled oily sand into buckets. They rushed to clean up areas before animals arrived to mate or give birth.

Workers did all they could. But oil-soaked beaches are hard to clean.

People sprayed hot water over rocks and sand. They used small machines like car wash wands. The hidden oil was forced out into the water, caught in booms, and sucked up with a big machine. But it wasn't enough.

After about four months, plans changed. Huge hot water heaters and high-pressure pumps took over. Workers blasted the beaches with hot water. The water hit harder than a fire hose. This cleaned up some of the oil. But hot water was hard on sea creatures and plants.

Workers cleaned beaches and shores for the following four years. But nature and time will need to do the rest.

Effects on Wildlife

The *Exxon Valdez* spilled at a bad time of year. In the sea, tiny plants and animals called *plankton* had bloomed. Plankton is food for millions of ocean creatures. Baby salmon were released from **hatcheries.** Herring returned to **spawn.** Hungry deer came to the beaches to nibble plants. Grizzly bears and black bears came out of winter dens. Birds were nesting. Seals and sea lions were having pups. Whales were migrating. New life was everywhere. What happened to all of it when the oil spilled?

Sea Otters

Oil spills are deadly to sea otters. Over 5,000 Alaskan sea otters died. They swallowed oil. They breathed the poisonous fumes. They ate clams **contaminated** with oil. They died when their fur was coated with oil.

A sea otter's fur is its survival suit. These sea mammals have thicker fur than any animal. How thick is it? They have 650,000 to 1 million hairs per square inch.

A sea otter's dense fur traps air. This helps keep cold water away from its skin. Otters get air next to their skin by grooming. They roll around. They rub, scrub, comb, and fluff with their paws.

> **How thick is a sea otter's fur?**
>
> A human has 60 hairs per square inch on the body. A human head has 20,000 hairs on it.

When the tips of an otter's fur get wet, they cling together in a waterproof layer. An otter's skin is never wet if its fur is clean. Staying warm and dry is how they survive in cold water.

What happens to sea otters when black, sticky oil floods their watery home? Try as he might, an otter cannot lick his fur clean. Licking the oily fur makes otters sick. No amount of rubbing and fluffing will trap air in his fur. He can no longer keep warm and dry.

Mothers may not recognize their oily pups. The pups may refuse to nurse from oiled mothers. The otters get sick and die. Often, they freeze or starve to death.

After the Exxon spill, people set up rescue centers to help save sea otters. Charlie Crangle is a fifth-grade teacher in Seward, Alaska. He helped at Exxon's otter cleanup center in Seward.

He says, "At first, the birds and otters were mixed. It was chaos. Nothing like this had ever happened before. We were waiting for experts to come and give advice. It made us sad and angry. The animals desperately needed help."

People worked fast. They quickly built a separate otter **rehabilitation** center. The otters arrived by helicopter and boat. Some came in cardboard boxes brought by caring people.

Charlie tells about the work. "It took eight or nine people three hours to wash an otter. We would hose it down, suds it up with dishwashing detergent, and rinse it off. Two to five times.

"Then we dried the otter with hair dryers. The drying took just as long as the washing. The otters got frisky as the **sedation** wore off. Then it was like trying to handle a wolverine."

Workers wore leather gloves up to their elbows. The gloves protected them from frightened otters that bit or clawed.

Some otters survived. But many sea otter pups had not yet learned the skills to stay alive. They could not be let go.

Four sea otter orphans from the Valdez oil spill went to live at Shedd Aquarium in Chicago. Rocky Point Reserve at Sea World in California became home to a few others.

Nine years after the spill, Charlie still thinks of the otters when he smells dishwashing detergent.

What does Charlie hope people learned from the oil spill?

"Oil spills are avoidable," he says. "We make choices. As a result, we put nature at risk because of human error."

Birds

How do oil spills hurt birds? Birds stay warm by trapping air between different layers of feathers. Oil sticks feathers together. Then they can't trap air anymore. In places like Alaska, that means birds will freeze to death.

Oil also makes birds so heavy that they can't float or fly. Many sink under the water and drown.

Swallowing oil poisons birds. They may stop laying eggs. Or they may lay eggs that do not hatch. Their young may not develop right.

Jessica Porter was a veterinarian at the Bird Rescue Center after the big spill. She tells what it must have been like for the birds. She says to imagine being captured by aliens and scrubbed in a bath. That's terror!

The terror begins when oil coats a bird's feathers. It lasts until the animal is finally freed. Or it dies.

"Think about it," says Jessica in a newspaper interview. "First, the bird is crammed into a net. Then it's stuffed into a box or bag. It has food crammed down its throat. It's put into a hot washtub and scrubbed while being held down by people. The bird doesn't understand we're trying to help."

She continues. "After washing, the bird is put into a sink and rinsed with a jet spray. Then it's thrown into a blow-dryer, picked up again and banded. When you consider all the birds have to go through, the cleanup is a survival test in itself."

Birds that survived the spill and the rescue were later returned to the wild. Even then, they may not survive. One worker says, "We like to set them free right away. Or they get sick and die just from being around people."

Some **species** waited many weeks to be set free. Some nested in the spill area. They would have gone right back to where they were found. They might get re-oiled. So they were held until the area was cleaned or the nesting season ended.

What if a bird had no chance for recovery?

Jessica explains, "There's no reason for it to keep suffering. We put those birds to sleep painlessly. With a shot to the heart or abdomen, they're dead within seconds."

There's no way to guess the number of birds that died. There were thousands. The number was impossible to count.

Jessica says, "Birds don't stick around long after they die. They sink. Or they're eaten."

Land Animals

Eagles, deer, and bears don't live in the water. But spills can still make them sick or kill them. Oiled animals mix into the **food chain.** Dead, oiled birds on beaches are dangerous to other animals. Eagles, ravens, bears, and foxes can be poisoned by eating them.

When deer eat oil-soaked grass, the oil coats their stomachs. They can't digest food. They starve to death. The same happens to eagles, foxes, and bears who eat oiled fish.

It's hard to keep animals from the path of an oil spill. *Exxon Valdez* workers tried. They learned a few things along the way.

For example, after the *Kuroshima* spill in 1997, helpers used noisemakers. The noise kept birds and animals away from the spill. It saved some lives. But many were still lost.

Everyone felt grief and anxiety. They wanted to do something to help.

Students helped. They cleaned towels used by workers. Students and teachers placed sandbags and logs to keep the oil slick from flowing into a nearby bay. High school students cleaned oil-soaked birds. Math students even figured out how long it would take the spilled oil to run like water through a kitchen faucet. The answer? Nine years!

Children could phone in questions to a team of experts. Government leaders, fishermen, Coast Guard members, and others answered their questions about the oil spill.

How did the oil spill affect the native peoples of Alaska? Many native villages in Alaska were hit hard. Their way of life depends on a stable environment.

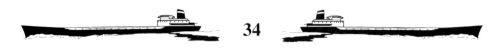

Walter Meganack is chief of the Port Graham tribe. His words were in the *Anchorage Daily News* after the *Exxon Valdez* spill.

Excerpt from the *Anchorage Daily News*, August 5, 1989

"The Native story is different from white man's story of oil devastation. It is different because our lives are different, what we value is different; how we see the water and land, the plants and the animals, is different. What white men do for sport and recreation and money, we do for life: for the life of our bodies, for the life of our spirits, and for the life of our ancient culture.

"It was early in the springtime. No fish yet. No snails yet. But the signs were with us. The green was starting. Some birds were flying and singing. The excitement of the season had just begun. And then we heard the news. Oil in the water. Lots of oil. Killing lots of water. It is too shocking to understand. Never in the millennium of our tradition have we thought it possible for the water to die. But it is true.

"We walk our beaches. But the snails and the barnacles and the chitons are falling off the rocks. Dead. Dead water. We caught our first fish, the annual first fish, the traditional delight of all—but it got sent to the state to be tested for oil. No first fish this year. We walk our beaches. But instead of gathering life, we gather death. Dead birds. Dead otters. Dead seaweed.

"People are angry. And afraid and confused. Our elders feel helpless. They cannot work on cleanup. They cannot do all the activities of gathering food and preparing for winter. And most of all, they cannot teach the young ones the Native ways. How will the children learn the values and the ways if the water is dead.

"We will need much help, much listening in order to live through the long barren season of dead water, a longer winter than before. . .We have never lived through this kind of death. But we have lived through lots of other kinds of death. We will learn from the past, we will learn from each other, and we will live."

The dead animals, sea life, and plants broke down into **hydrogen** and **carbon.** These are the two parts, or *elements,* that form oil, natural gas, and coal. These are called *fossil fuels* because of how they form. Fossil fuels heat our homes and run our cars.

Some of the world's largest oil deposits lie under the deserts of the Middle East. The Middle East holds two-thirds of the world's known oil supply. And about one-fourth of the world's oil comes from beneath the ocean floor.

Demand for oil has grown over the years. Today, oil is the number one resource used in the world. So people had to figure out how to move oil to the places that need it.

How Oil Is Moved

Early Days

In 1859, E. L. Drake drilled the first modern oil well. It was near Titusville, Pennsylvania. Since then, people have faced a problem. And that's getting oil from the well to where we can use it.

In the early days, oil was shipped in wooden barrels. Wagons hauled them on land. Barges moved them on water. Spills were common. They were a bother. But they didn't seem to be a danger.

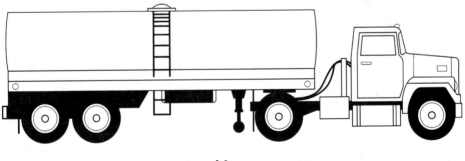

Now

Ships, trucks, and pipelines carry crude oil across land. They carry the crude oil to refineries.

Chapter

Why Do We Need Oil?

Oil can be deadly to the environment. But it is important to the U.S. **economy.** Without oil, life today would be very different for all of us. What would your world be like without CDs or in-line skates? Can you imagine not having rubber tires and two-liter soda bottles? They are all **petroleum-based** products.

People around the world use nearly 6,000 petroleum-based products. People, cars, trucks, industries, jets, and homes all need oil. A jumbo jet burns as much as 3,335 gallons of jet fuel in an hour.

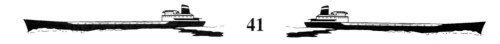

Products Made from Oil

The *refining* process changes oil into other useful products. Crude oil is heated and sent to a special tower. It's called a *fractionating* tower. Fractionating means separating. Inside, the crude oil is turned into useful products.

Here are some examples.
- motor oil and gasoline for cars
- diesel fuel for heavy trucks and trains
- bunker fuel for ships
- heating oil to warm buildings in winter
- asphalt to make roads

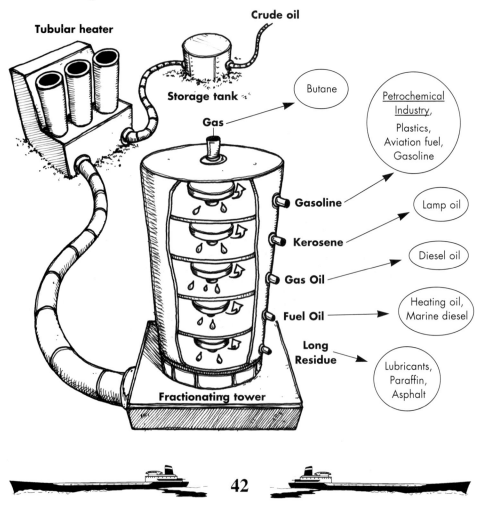

There's oil right under your nose too. It's in the carpet on your floor, the paint on your walls, and the plastic in toys. All these things probably contain oil.

If you have a gas stove at home, it uses natural gas. So do gas grills, fireplaces, clothes dryers, and water heaters.

You might even be wearing oil. Many fabrics are made of artificial fibers. These fibers contain chemicals from oil.

How much oil do you use?

How many times a day do you use something that runs on oil? Or something made from oil? Think about it. You'll probably be surprised by your answer!

Oil Power

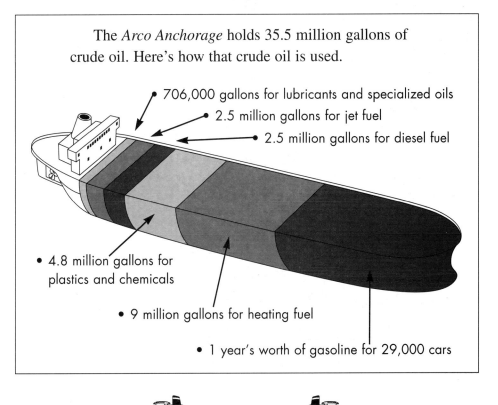

The *Arco Anchorage* holds 35.5 million gallons of crude oil. Here's how that crude oil is used.

- 706,000 gallons for lubricants and specialized oils
- 2.5 million gallons for jet fuel
- 2.5 million gallons for diesel fuel
- 4.8 million gallons for plastics and chemicals
- 9 million gallons for heating fuel
- 1 year's worth of gasoline for 29,000 cars

OPEC

Since 1973, a group of nations has controlled the price and distribution of oil around the world. It is called the Organization of Petroleum Exporting Countries (OPEC). Members include the following.

Latin America—Ecuador, Venezuela

Middle East—Iran, Iraq, Kuwait, Qatar, Saudi Arabia, United Arab Emirates

Africa—Algeria, Libya, Gabon, Algeria

Southeast Asia—Indonesia

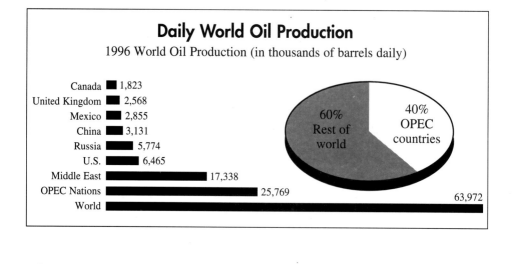

Daily World Oil Production

1996 World Oil Production (in thousands of barrels daily)

Canada	1,823
United Kingdom	2,568
Mexico	2,855
China	3,131
Russia	5,774
U.S.	6,465
Middle East	17,338
OPEC Nations	25,769
World	63,972

60% Rest of world

40% OPEC countries

Oil for the Future

How will world oil supply keep up with demand? It will take imports as well as new discoveries. Where will future oil come from? It's not an easy question. There are lots of things to think about. These include land, wildlife, and money.

Here are some possible answers.

The Arctic National Wildlife Refuge

The Arctic National Wildlife Refuge (A.N.W.R.) is a huge piece of land in the frozen north of Alaska. It is about the size of Indiana. Polar bears, grizzlies, wolves, foxes, caribou, fish, and many plants live there. Birds from six continents flock there to raise their young. There are native peoples who live there. Otherwise, it is almost untouched by humans.

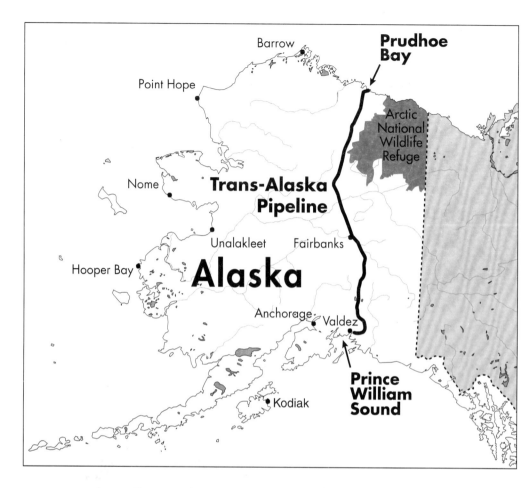

According to scientists, there may be a lot of oil in the A.N.W.R. The oil is under the ice at the edge of the Beaufort Sea. It may be more than half the undiscovered oil in the U.S. But no one can know for sure until they look. Some think there may be enough oil to supply 10 percent of the nation's fuel—for the next 20 years!

The United States imports over half of the oil it uses. Many people feel that the U.S. should not depend so much on other countries for oil. These people want to use the oil from the A.N.W.R. They want to build a pipeline across the refuge. The pipeline would carry the oil to southern Alaska just like the Trans-Alaska pipeline.

Environmentalists warn that we should leave the A.N.W.R. alone. They fear that the land would be damaged during pipeline construction. They fear that an oil spill might hurt the ocean and wildlife.

Oil companies argue with the environmentalists. They say exploring and drilling for wells would do little damage.

The National Petroleum Reserve-Alaska

The National Petroleum Reserve-Alaska (NPR-A) is another huge piece of the Arctic. Will the government open this piece of the Arctic to look for oil?

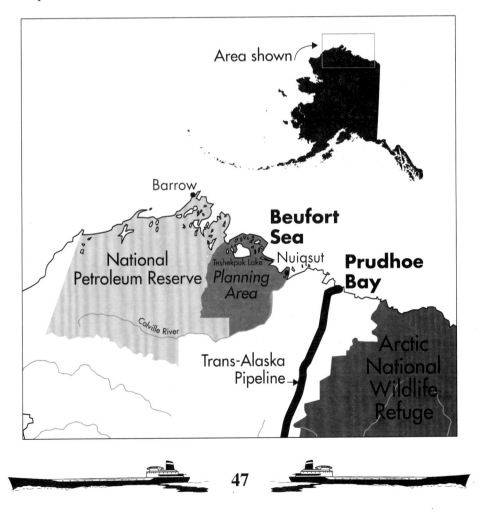

A federal agency spent most of 1997 making plans for oil leasing. Congress will vote on it. An act of Congress is required before development in the National Petroleum Reserve-Alaska is allowed.

The oil industry is already on Prudhoe Bay. But they want to keep the crude oil flowing through the Trans-Alaska Pipeline.

Conservation leaders say America's Arctic is more important. They say its natural state is valuable. It is even more valuable than the oil that may be locked deep in the land.

The debate is the same as in the A.N.W.R, except for one big difference. The NPR-A was set aside in 1923 to be a petroleum reserve. The law says that the oil should be used only to meet the total energy needs of the nation.

Does the U.S. need the oil? Tapping reserve oil could make the U.S. more self-sufficient. But right now, the U.S. doesn't use all the oil coming out of Alaska. Some is exported.

Those against drilling say that the U.S. should not pump the oil out now. The U.S. should not sell oil to other countries now. Currently oil is relatively cheap and plentiful. People say that in 30 years, the U.S. would just have to buy it back at twice the price.

But the U.S. wouldn't be able to get back any wilderness that was lost—not at any price.

Should we use the oil under the A.N.W.R. or the NPR-A? This is a big decision. How will oil development affect wildlife? How will it affect the native peoples who live off the wildlife?

Few issues have simple solutions. They often cause storms of protest. Knowing all sides of an issue is important. It can help you make good choices when it is your time to vote.

Changing the Way We Produce Energy

Many people are trying to use less oil and gas. Here are three good reasons why.

1. They're expensive to use.
2. They are limited resources that can be used up.
3. They pollute, spill, and harm living things.

More places are changing the ways they produce energy. There's plenty of energy that doesn't pollute and won't get used up.

People around the globe are working hard to bring it to your home. They use more wind, water, and solar power instead of oil to make energy.

Some companies make cars that don't use gasoline. These engines collect sunlight. They convert it into steady electrical power to run the car.

Watch for more new energy ideas.

Chapter 6

Prevention:
Our Best Hope

Modern cleanup methods do wonders. Yet there is still no foolproof way to clean up an oil spill. Oil cleanups can harm the environment too.

The only real solution is prevention.

Large oil tankers leaving Valdez now have two towboats, or *tugs,* that go with them. Each tug carries special oil-spill equipment. In case of spills, they are ready at a moment's notice.

Special Harbor Pilots go aboard tankers. They carefully guide full oil tankers past Bligh Reef. That's the reef that sliced the *Exxon Valdez.* Local villagers help decide how oil should be transported.

The *Exxon Valdez* oil spill set new tanker laws in motion. These laws make oil shipping safer. The Oil Pollution Act of 1990 was written to help prevent spills.

The Oil Pollution Act of 1990

The Oil Pollution Act of 1990 (O.P.A.) made laws tougher. The O.P.A. made tankers and their owners responsible for cleaning up the oil they spill.

- Ships must have written Emergency Response Plans. These plans tell how they will clean up an oil spill fast. And their owners must know how to act quickly and properly.
- All spills over 10 gallons must be reported.
- All ships must carry insurance for cleaning up a spill they cause.
- All oil tankers must have double hulls (bottoms with two layers of metal) by the year 2015.
- And all new ships must be built with double hulls.

O.P.A. has helped make oil transportation safer. But it still is not enough.

Oil-Spill Drills

Many oil companies are taking matters into their own hands. They perform oil-spill drills regularly. All employees that work around oil must take part.

Workers know when some drills will happen. Other drills are a surprise.

During some drills, workers practice getting equipment up and ready. Other times, they must get equipment and clean up the spill at a record pace.

A fake spill is set up. They often dump a truckload of oranges, which float like oil. As the oranges start to drift with the current, workers act quickly. They bring out the booms.

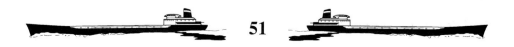

They need to contain as many oranges as possible. They must work fast. They are watched, timed, and "graded" on their performance.

Prevention Schools

People who work for oil companies attend other classes. Some learn about hazardous materials. They call this HAZWOPER training (Hazardous Waste Operations and Emergency Response).

Workers learn the best ways to prevent different kinds of spills. They learn what to do when a spill occurs. They learn whom to call. They learn who is at risk from the spill.

Trained workers must be ready for spills on water and on land. They must prepare for spills from tankers in the ocean, storage tanks in towns or cities, and leaky underground storage tanks. They must even be ready for spills at gas station pumps.

This training is very important. The O.P.A. expects all oil companies to know how to prevent and respond to oil spills.

This is a tough rule. Some say it is like expecting each of us to know how to fight our own fires. But it's important that the right people are well trained. A poorly handled oil spill can be as damaging as one that is not handled at all.

Spending for Prevention

Oil companies spend millions of dollars in prevention. They know that oil spills affect a company's image. They want to improve tanker safety and prevent expensive accidents.

Some money goes to new tankers. Some goes to improve crew training. Properly trained crews make fewer mistakes. Some is used to hire more crew members. With more crew members, workers won't get so tired. There's less chance for

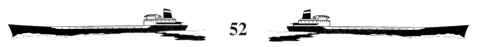

members, workers won't get so tired. There's less chance for human error.

Companies are checking the age of their ships. The president of Conoco Shipping Company says, "The average age of many fleets is growing older and older."

Conoco has pledged to have only double-hulled tankers in its fleet by the year 2000.

Oil-Spill Organizations

Each year, several oil groups have a big meeting. Members come from many countries. They all want to make oil shipping safer. These are some groups working to stop oil spills.

- American Petroleum Institute
- Environmental Protection Agency
- U.S. Coast Guard
- International **Maritime** Organization
- International Petroleum Industry Environmental Conservation Association

Learning from the Past

The harm from a large oil spill seems unthinkable. Lives are lost. Dreams are crushed. Livelihoods are ruined. And environments are damaged beyond repair.

But we can learn from an oil spill. Disasters make us think. Sometimes, good changes can come from bad oil spills.

The Alaska Sea Life Center is a good thing. It is a result of the *Exxon Valdez* oil spill. Exxon set aside funds after the oil spill. The money was to help restore wildlife and marine habitats hurt by the spill.

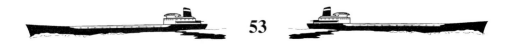

The Alaska Sea Life Center opened in 1998. It was built
with Exxon money, plus public and private donations. The
purpose of the Alaska Sea Life Center is to study cold-water
marine life in Alaska. It is the first Arctic research aquarium of
its kind in the western hemisphere.

The Alaska Sea Life Center was built on Resurrection Bay
in Seward. Seward was one of the care sites for oiled animals
after the *Exxon Valdez* spill. Resurrection Bay is a good place
for the Sea Life Center. It is home to many kinds of marine
creatures.

Marine animals and sea birds that are sick or injured will
live in the Sea Life Center while they get well. Researchers
from around the world will come. They will study the animals
to learn about their habits and homes.

The Center is well-equipped. In wet labs, animals move around in sea water. Scientists study what happens as the sick animals get well.

In dry labs, scientists look at samples under microscopes. They research diseases to help ailing animal populations. And X-rays and surgeries are done in a special animal care unit.

The Alaska Sea Life Center will help if another oil-spill disaster ever happens. It will be ready to give rescue care and recovery support. Meanwhile, the Center will help people learn more about marine animals.

Important Lessons

Every time we spill oil, we learn. And every time we learn, rules change. The 1997 *Kuroshima* spill taught another lesson. Freighters and cruise ships do not have the same rules as tankers that carry oil. But they may carry up to half a million gallons of fuel.

Some think that similar rules should apply to freighters and cruise ships. Will this spill make our waters safer by changing laws again?

We can keep learning. Laws can keep changing. Companies can invent safer practices. And they can use funds to find answers that help make shipping oil less dangerous to all living things.

We're All in This Together

It's easy to blame oil companies. But the truth is, we all use too much oil.

Large oil spills are just one way oil pollutes the environment. Are you surprised to learn that more oil is spilled by ordinary people than by oil tankers? People everywhere spill oil. Some dump used oil in alleys or on the ground. Some fail

to keep their cars, boats, and motorcycles in good condition. Then they leak oil. These spills are more difficult to detect than large oil spills.

Spills like these can create more problems than we think. In 1983, 350 million gallons of oil were spilled. This oil was not spilled by one tanker in one location. This oil was spilled by thousands of people across the nation. It was spilled by ordinary people doing ordinary things. They failed to dispose of their oil properly. This oil was almost 32 times the amount of oil spilled in Prince William Sound.

It doesn't take much oil to cause trouble. One pint (2 cups) creates a one-acre slick. That's the size of a football field! Just a tiny bit of oil spoils the taste and smell of drinking water. Just 2 pints (4 cups) of oil will spoil 125,000 gallons of drinking water. That's more water than 15 people drink in a lifetime!

You Can Make a Difference!

One way to stop oil spills is to use less oil. Here's a short list of things with oil in them that people use. Can you cut back on anything?

ballpoint pens	acrylic sweaters	model cars	wax crayons
paintbrushes	beach balls	nail polish	balloons
guitar strings	transparent tape	plastic trash bags	volleyballs

We can also work to save energy. The less energy we use, the less oil we use. The less oil we use, the less we need to ship. That means fewer tankers in the oceans. The chances of spills will decrease.

Here's what you can do to use less energy from oil, gas, and coal.

- Keep the heat as low as you can. Almost half of all the energy used in homes is for heat.
- Stop using the car so much. Walk or ride your bike when you travel short distances.
- Keep the refrigerator door closed until you know what you want.
- Check for cracks or holes in your home where heat escapes. Then help cover them up.
- Turn off lights when you're not using them.
- Wash out and reuse plastic bags.
- Dispose of oil properly. Take waste oil to service stations or collection sites for recycling. Oily rags or clothing can be washed and used again. Other oily stuff can be kept in metal containers. Save them for spring community cleanups or hazardous-waste pickups. Never throw oily waste into landfills. It will seep into underwater drinking supplies. Hardware stores sell oil-absorbing pads you can use to get all the oil out of water before you pour it down a drain.

Your own ideas count too! During the *Exxon Valdez* oil spill, many people had ideas for cleanup. Some examples include using chicken feathers to soak up the oil and sprinkling powdered cheese on the oil. That made it easier to pick up.

You can help by learning all you can about your environment. Learn how your actions affect other living things. And use what you learn to help make good decisions. Help make land and water safer for all living things.

A Final Note

Robert Barnwell is a teacher in Dutch Harbor, Alaska. This town was affected by the *Kuroshima* oil spill in November 1997.

He says, "Realize that you will be inheriting this world. Do you want to continue to live with the risks? Can you live with the fact that oil spills will continue to happen? Can you live with the fact that oceans will continue to become polluted?

"If not, here is your challenge. Picture another way to live free of oil. Think of ways to get beyond the oil reliance without big changes to your quality of life. How can you help prevent oil spills?"

GLOSSARY

anchor	device (usually metal) that is attached to a ship by a cable; helps hold ship in place when cast overboard
bacteria	tiny living things that occur in soil, water, and air; can cause disease
barge	flat-bottomed boat used to transport goods
boom	large floating curtains that are laid on the water to "corral" an oil spill
carbon	nonmetallic element found in such things as coal, petroleum, and asphalt
carbon dioxide	heavy, colorless gas
collision	when two or more objects, such as ships, come together with force; a crash
conservation	planned protection and preservation of natural resources
contaminated	soiled, spoiled, or infected
crude oil	thick, tar-like oil taken directly from underground; not yet processed for use
desalination	salt-removal process
double hull	two layers of metal on the bottom of a tanker rather than one thickness (single hull)
economy	structure of financial life in a country or area
environmentalist	one who actively works to preserve the environment
fertilizer	substance added to soil to help it grow plant life

food chain	structure of living creatures—from the biggest life forms to the smallest; each life form uses the one below it as its food source
freighter	ship used to carry goods
grounding	when a ship runs onto land, the ocean bottom, or rock formations in shallow water
habitat	place where an animal or a plant lives and grows
hydrogen	nonmetallic element; usually a colorless, odorless gas
industry	manufacturing and business activity as a whole
maritime	of or relating to the sea
microbes	tiny plants or animals
natural gas	a fossil fuel gas found with underground crude oil reserves
navigation	the science of getting ships from place to place
petroleum	an oily liquid found in the earth; used to create gasoline, kerosene, diesel oil, and other products
petroleum-based	made from oil
pipeline	line of pipe with pumps and other control devices for moving liquids and gases
pollution	a human-caused, harmful change in air, water, or soil

ramming	crashing
recycle	to take apart, or break down, used products and then reuse the parts or materials
refinery	place where oil is refined or made free of unwanted materials
rehabilitation	process of restoring an animal to a good condition
sedation	state produced by using a drug that relaxes and eases pain
silt	type of sandy soil usually found near a river
skimmer	vacuum-like equipment that sucks oil from the surface of water
slick	oily patch formed on the top of the water after an oil spill
spawn	to produce eggs
species	biological category of living creatures
tanker	a large marine ship used to carry huge quantities of petroleum
toxic	poisonous to humans or animals

Index